CONTENTS

INTRODUCTION

So, you love smoking weed and live in a state where growing your own weed is perfectly legal? Then, what are you waiting for? It's time to learn how to grow marijuana in the comfort of your own home! One of the reasons why people are discouraged from growing their own cannabis plant is that they believe it to be a costly, complicated, and time-consuming project when in reality it is not so. Sure, there are challenges, but if you follow these simple steps, you will learn all you need to know to grow the best and most potent buds. Plus, you get the added satisfaction of consuming something you've grown yourself. And isn't that a reward in itself?

In this book, you will learn how to measure the dimensions of your grow area, what ventilation, airflow, tools, and equipment you must have, how to set up your grow space properly, how to germinate your seeds, using germination pot technique, how to look after your seedlings, in the seedling stage, how to implement the three most sufficient cannabis training methods called the bend & secure technique, super cropping, and the screen of green, how to set up the vegetative lighting schedule, how to provide nutrients to your plants.

MARIJUANA CULTIVATION

Cannabis belongs to the genus Cannabis in the family Cannabaceae may include three species, Cannabis indica, Cannabis sativa, and Cannabis ruderalis, (APG II system) or one variable species. It is typically a dioecious (each individual is either male or female) annual plant. C. sativa and C. indica generally grow tall, with some varieties reaching 4 metres, or 13 feet. Female plants produce tetrahydrocannabinol (THC) (up to 31% by weight) as the season changes from summer to autumn. C. ruderalis is very short, produces only trace amounts of THC, but is very rich in cannabidiol (CBD), which may be 40% of the cannabinoids in a plant and is an antagonist to THC, and it flowers independently of the photoperiod and according to age. However, commercial cross-bred hybrids containing both ruderalis, indica and/or sativa genes exist (usually called autoflowering).

CULTIVATION REQUIREMENTS

Cannabis needs certain conditions to flourish.

Growth medium

Soil is required, except for cannabis grown with hydroponics or aeroponics.

Sufficient nutrients — commercial potting soils usually indicate this as "N-P-K = x%-y%-z%". This indicates the percentages of fundamental nutritional elements, i.e., nitrogen, phosphorus and potassium. Nutrients are often provided to the soil via fertilizers but such practice requires caution[citation needed].

A soil pH between 5.8 and 6.5. This value can be adjusted – see soil pH. Commercial fertilizers (even organic) tend to make the soil more acidic.

Warmth

The optimal day temperature range for cannabis is 24 to 30 °C (75 to 86 °F). Temperatures above 31 °C (88 °F) and below 15.5 °C (60 °F) seem to decrease THC potency and slow growth. At 13 °C (55 °F) the plant undergoes a mild shock, though some strains withstand frost temporarily.

Light

Light can be natural (outdoor growing) or artificial (indoor growing). Under artificial light, the plant typically remains under a regime of 16–24 hours of light and 0–8 hours of darkness from the germination until flowering, with longer light periods being conducive to vegetative growth, and longer dark periods being conducive to flowering. However, generally cannabis only requires thirteen hours of continuous light to remain in the vegetative stage. The 'Gas Lantern Routine' is an alternate lighting schedule that has proven to be successful for growing cannabis, while saving a significant amount of energy. For optimal health, cannabis plants require a period of light and a period of dark. It has been suggested that, when subjected to a regimen of constant light without a dark period, cannabis begins to show signs of decreased photosynthetic response, lack of vigor, and an overall decrease in vascular development. Typically, flowering is induced by providing at least 12 hours per day of complete darkness. Flowering in cannabis is triggered by a hormonal reaction within the plant that is initiated by an increase in length of its dark cycle, i.e. the plant needs sufficient prolonged darkness for bract/bracteole (flowering) to begin. Some Indica varieties require as little as 8 hours of dark to begin flowering, whereas some Sativa varieties require up to 13 hours.

Water

Watering frequency and amount is determined by many factors, including temperature and light, the age, size and stage of growth of the plant and the medium's ability to retain water. A conspicuous sign of water problems is the wilting of leaves. Giving too much water can kill cannabis plants if the growing medium gets over-saturated. This is mainly due to oxygen not being able to enter the root system. Anaerobic bacteria start to accumulate due to waterlogged, stale conditions. They begin to consume plant roots, beneficial (aerobic) bacteria, as well as nutrients and fertilizer. When using soil as a growth medium, the soil should be allowed to dry down adequately before re-watering.

Humidity

Humidity is an important part of plant growth. Dry conditions slow the rate of photosynthesis. Ideal levels of humidity for optimal growth are 40–60% RH.

Nutrients

Nutrients are taken up from the soil by roots. Nutrient soil amendments (fertilizers) are added when the soil nutrients are depleted. Fertilizers can be chemical or organic, liquid or powder, and usually contain a mixture of ingredients. Commercial fertilizers indicate the levels of NPK (nitrogen, phosphorus, and potassium). In general, cannabis needs more N than P and K during all life phases. The presence of secondary nutrients (calcium, magnesium, sulfur) is recommended. Micronutrients (e.g. iron, boron, chlorine, manganese, copper, zinc, molybdenum) rarely manifest as deficiencies.

Because cannabis' nutrient needs vary widely depending on the variety, they are usually determined by trial and error and fertilizers are applied sparingly to avoid burning the plant.

STAGES OF DEVELOPMENT

Germination

Germination is the process by which a seed sprouts and a root emerges. Germination in cannabis can occur in as little as twelve hours or can take as long as eight days, depending on the cultivar and environmental conditions. Warmth, darkness, and moisture initiate metabolic processes such as the activation of hormones that trigger the expansion of the embryo within the seed. Then the seed coat cracks open and a small embryonic root emerges and begins growing downward (because of gravitropism), if placed in a proper growing medium. Soon (after 2–4 days) the root is anchored and two oval cotyledons (sometimes called "false leaves" or "seed leaves") emerge in search of light and the remains of the seed shell are pushed away. This marks the beginning of the seedling stage.

Germination is initiated by soaking seeds either between wet paper towels, in a cup of water at room temperature, in wet peat pellets, or directly in potting soil. Peat pellets are often used as a germinating medium because the saturated pellets with their seedlings can be planted directly into the intended growing medium with a minimum of shock to the plant.

Seedling phase

A very young C. sativa seedling. The tips of the first set of rough leaves are emerging between the two round seed leaves (cotyledons)

The seedling stage begins when the seed coat splits open and exposes the root and cotyledons. It lasts from 1 to 4 weeks and is the period of greatest vulnerability in the life cycle of the plant, requiring moderate humidity levels, medium to high light intensity, and adequate but not excessive soil moisture. Most indoor growers use compact fluorescent or T5 fluorescent lights during this stage as they produce little heat. HPS and MH lights produce large amounts of radiant heat and increase the rate of transpiration in the plant which can quickly dry out seedlings with their small root systems.

Vegetative phase

This cannabis plant is being grown in a coco coir medium. It is only making stems and leaves at this point because it is in the vegetative stage

Duration: 1–2 months indoors. In this stage the plant needs a significant amount of light and nutrients, depending on the genetics of the particular plant. It continues to grow vertically and produce new leaves. The sex is starting to reveal itself, which is a sign that the next stage begins. Concurrently the root system expands downwards in search of more water and food.

When the plant possesses seven sets of true leaves and the 8th is barely visible in the center of the growth tip, or shoot apical meristem (SAM), the plant has entered the vegetative phase of growth. During the vegetative phase, the plant directs its energy resources primarily to the growth of leaves, stems, and roots. A strong root system is required for strong floral development. A plant needs 1 or 2 months to mature before blooming. The plant is ready when it has revealed its sex. Plant size is a good indicator of sex. Females tend to be shorter and branchier due to their raceme type inflorescence than males, whose flowers grow in panicles. The males are then usually culled when they are identified, so that the females will not be pollinated, thus producing parthenocarpic fruits (popularly called "sinsemilla", meaning "without seed").

During the vegetative phase, cultivators generally employ an 18- to 24-hour photoperiod because the plants grow more quickly if they receive more light, although a warmer and cooler period are required for optimal health. Although no dark period is required, there is debate among cultivators as to whether a dark period is beneficial, and many continue to employ a dark period. Energy savings often support using a dark period, as plants undergo late day decline and therefore lighting during the late night hours is less effective.

The amount of time to grow a cannabis plant indoors in the vegetative stage depends on the size of the flower, the light used, the size of the space, and how many plants are intended to flower at once, and how big the strain gets in "the stretch" (i.e., the first two weeks of flowering).

Cannabis cultivators employ fertilizers high in nitrogen and potassium during the vegetative stage, as well as a complete micronutrient fertilizer. The strength of the fertilizer is gradually increased as the plants grow and become more hardy.

Advanced cultivation methods include:

Training and trellising techniques such as Screen of Green (also known as SCROG), Sea of Green (also known as SOG) "Super cropping" and LST super cropping; and entire systems and methods such as the NIMBY no-dump method, Hempy Bucket, and the Krusty Freedom Bucket methods. Research into the production of cannabis for the drug Marinol and other more profitable and marketable forms of cannabis-based medicines has further pushed the envelope of cannabis cultivation in all forms of laboratory, both public and private.

Using a water or air-based growth medium (known as hydroponics and aeroponics respectively)

The use of homemade, organic composted fertilizers

The emphasis on advanced cultivation techniques, as well as the availability of hybrid strains (with names like Northern Lights, Master Kush, NYC Diesel), is believed to be a factor in the increase in the overall quality and variety of commercially available cannabis over the past few decades. The Internet in particular has brought together widely diverse genetics from around the world through trading and purchasing. However, well-grown heirloom strains (e.g. island sweet skunk, fruity Thai etc.) are used to produce 1 gram per watt (g/W) harvest.

Pre-flowering phase

A young male cannabis plant during early flowering stage

Also called the stretch, this takes one day to two weeks. Most plants spend 10–14 days in this period after switching the light cycle to 12 hours of darkness. Plant development increases dramatically, with the plant doubling or more in size. (See reproductive development below.) Production of more branches and nodes occurs during this stage, as the structure for flowering grows. The plant starts to develop bracts/bracteoles where the branches meet the stem (nodes). Pre-flowering indicates the plant is ready to flower.

Flowering and fruition phases

The flowering phase varies from about 6 to 12 weeks for pure indicas with their shorter flowering time than pure sativas. Mixed indica/sativa strains have an intermediate flowering time. The sex is clearly revealed in the first phase, the actual flowering. Males produce little ball-like flowers clustered together like grapes called panicles. Most plants (except auto flowering strains that flower independently of photoperiod) begin to flower under diminishing light. In nature, cannabis plants sense the forthcoming winter as the Earth revolves about the Sun and daylight reduces in duration (see also season). The next phase consists in the fruition (or fruiting): the females inflorescences that were not pollinated (i.e.: fertilized by male pollen) start to produce infructescences that contain sticky white resin-containing glands (or trichomes) in a final attempt for pollination by windborne male pollen. The trichomes produce resins that contain the largest amounts of THC and CBN, the two main psychoactive substances. Fertilized females continue to produce resinous trichomes but more plant energy is consumed by the production of seeds, which can be half the mass of a fertilized bract; thus, to maximize resin per gram, infertile cultivation is preferred.

Inflorescence that produce no seeds are called sin semilla (which translates to "without seeds" in Spanish, and is often misspelled as one word). Potent sin semilla is especially important to medical users, to minimize the amount of cannabis they must consume to be afforded relief. Cannabis with seeds is generally considered to be of inferior quality and/or grown with inferior technique.

The budding fruits of a male cannabis plant

Cannabis grown is induced into flowering by decreasing its photoperiod to at least 10 hours of darkness per day. In order to initiate a flowering response, the number of hours of darkness must exceed a critical point. Generally the more hours of darkness each day, the shorter the overall flowering period but the lower the yield. Conversely, the fewer hours of darkness each day, the longer the overall flowering period and the higher the yield. Traditionally, most growers change their plants lighting cycle to 12 hours on and 12 hours off since this works as a happy medium to which most strains respond well. This change in photoperiod mimics the plant's natural outdoor cycle, with up to 18 hours of light per day in the summer and down to less than 12 hours of light in fall and winter.[citation needed] Some 'semi-autoflowering' strains that have been bred exclusively for outdoor use, particularly in outdoor climates such as that of the UK, will start flowering with as much as 16–17 hours of light per day. Usually they can start flowering in July and finish far earlier than other strains, particularly those that haven't been bred as outdoor strains. Semi-autoflowering strains can be harvested before the weather in northern latitudes becomes very wet and cold (generally October), whereas other strains are just finishing flowering, and may suffer from botrytis (grey mold) caused by wet weather. Alternatively growers may artificially induce the flowering period during the warmer months by blacking out the plants for 12 hours a day i.e. by covering the plants with black plastic for example, which excludes all light during this period so the plant can flower even during long days.

Although the flowering hormone in most plants (including cannabis) is present during all phases of growth, it is inhibited by exposure to light. To induce flowering, the plant must be subject to at least 8 hours of darkness per day; this number is very strain-specific and most growers use 12 hours of darkness.

Flowers from certain plants (e.g. cannabis) are called bract/bracteole, and are (with cannabis) the most prized part of the plant. During the late period, the bract/bracteole are easily visible to the naked eye. Bract/bracteole development begins approximately 1–2 weeks after the photoperiod is reduced. In the first weeks of flowering a plant usually doubles in size and can triple. Bract/bracteole development ends around 5 weeks into flowering and is followed by a period of bract/bracteole "swelling". During this time the buds greatly increase in weight and size.

IMPORTANT THINGS TO KNOW BEFORE GROWING CANNABIS

Growing weed is exciting. Whether you use it recreationally or medicinally, there is something special about sewing your own seeds and harvesting your very own buds. But before you start your grow, it's important to keep a few things in mind.

UNDERSTAND THE BASICS OF CANNABIS

Before starting a cannabis grow, it's vital you have a solid understanding of the cannabis plant. While you don't need to be an expert on everything there is to know about weed plants, make sure you at least understand the basics of the plant's life cycle, nutrient requirements, and structure. Here are some must-know facts about cannabis to help you get started. Before you think about germinating your seeds, make sure to get your hands on a good marijuana grow book and continue reading through our backlog of grow:

Cannabis is a genus of flowering plants which can be either male, female, or hermaphrodite.

Cannabis plants can be grown indoors, outdoor, and in greenhouses.

In nature, male plants pollinate female flowers (or buds) to create new seeds. Most growers, however, will keep their females unpollinated to produce better buds.

There are 3 main varieties of cannabis; indica, sativa, and ruderalis. All 3 vary in morphology and effects.

Indica and sativa cannabis varieties are naturally photoperiod plants, meaning they flower based on how much light they receive. Ruderalis plants, on the other hand, flower automatically based on age, regardless of changes to their light cycles.

There are 3 main phases to the cannabis life cycle; seedling phase, vegetative phase, and flowering phase.

In nature, cannabis plants grow annually, usually beginning their life cycle between spring and the first days of summer. The length of a plant's life cycle can vary greatly (anywhere between 4-10 months).

KNOW HOW MUCH POWER YOU'LL NEED

Once you have a better understanding of the cannabis plant, it's important to realise how much power you'll need to keep your grow running. This mainly applies to indoor growers. Remember, cannabis plants need a lot of light (up to 18 hours per day minimum). In order to run a successful grow indoors, you'll need to power a quality grow light (most growers opt for 400-600W grow lights). Apart from your light, you'll also need to power other electrical equipment such as fans, extractors, and more. In some residential houses, this may cause a power overload, as residential power circuits are sometimes limited to roughly 1500w.

UNDERSTAND THE COSTS

We're not going to beat around the bush; growing weed costs money. And, depending on how professional you want to keep your grow op, you'll likely need to invest in some expensive equipment to get you started. The exact equipment you'll need to grow weed indoors will vary depending on your skills as a grower and the size of your grow. Nonetheless, most indoor growers will need at least the following equipment, as well as pots, soil, and other basic grow accessories;

• Grow light

• Fan

• Grow tent

• Air filter

• Light reflectors

• Small ventilator

• Timer

• pH meter

Buying this equipment and running it will obviously take a toll on your back pocket. However, most of the equipment you'll need to buy for your grow is reusable, and you'll usually make your money back after just a few harvests.

UNDERSTAND DIFFERENT GROW METHODS

Cannabis can be grown in many different ways. Before you start your grow, remember to read up on various grow methods and pick one that is best suited to your skill level and budget. Arguably the most common way to grow weed is in soil. When doing so, growers will add nutrients to the soil which the plant then absorbs via its roots. These nutrients can be provided via store-bought nutrient solutions or natural alternatives like compost. Alternatively, some advanced growers may opt to grow their plants in mediums other than soil. Methods that use mediums other than soil (such as coco coir, sand, water, or even misted air) are referred to as hydroponic methods. Deciding on which way to grow weed is completely up to you.

However, inexperienced growers are generally advised to start with simpler, soil-based methods.

PICK THE RIGHT GROW SPACE

Picking a grow space is an essential part of growing weed. You'll want to think about your grow space well before you start growing. You've essentially got 2 options for where to grow weed; indoors and outdoors. Both have their pros and cons. Growing outdoors is great because it allows you to avoid a lot of costs. After all, by harnessing the natural power of the sun, you won't need to buy a grow light. Plus, as long as your plants get a nice gentle breeze, you also won't need to install any fans or extractors. The major downfall to growing outdoors, however, is that you have no control over the climate and light exposure of your plants. Also, outdoor operations are likely to attract more attention, which may be problematic if you live in an area where the cultivation of cannabis is illegal.

Indoor growing also has its fair share of benefits. First and foremost, your plants will be out of plain sight and therefore less likely to attract any unwanted attention. Plus, you'll also have complete control over the climate in your grow space, allowing you to adjust things like temperature, humidity, and light hours to create the ideal environment for your plants. The major downfall to growing indoors, however, is the cost of buying and maintaining all the necessary equipment, as well as the increased costs of electricity. Growing indoors also means you'll have to deal with space restrictions.

UNDERSTAND THE SIGNS OF NUTRIENT DEFICIENCIES, PESTS, ETC

Cannabis, just like other plants, is susceptible to a variety of pests and diseases. Plus, the plant also has complex nutrient, light, and water requirements which, when not met properly, can affect the health of your plants and the size/quality of your harvest. Luckily, if you learn to identify the tell-tale signs of pest infestations, diseases, or nutrient deficiencies, you'll be able to treat them quickly and minimize their effect on your plants. Here are some common signs that there's something wrong with your plants:

Nutrient deficiencies: Signs include red stems, pale foliage, stunted growth, curling and/or spotted leaves, and or/malformations.

Pests/diseases: Signs include white spotted leaves (caused by bite marks), twisted leaves, curling leaves, yellow/brown spots on leaves and foliage, brown or black buds, white powder on foliage, and more.

UNDERSTAND PLANT NUTRIENTS

All plants need nutrients to survive and grow, and cannabis is no different. You'll want to know the basics of how and what to feed your plants before you start your grow. The 3 basic nutrients cannabis plants need to survive are nitrogen, phosphorus, and potassium (NPK). Most nutrients solutions will contain these compounds in varying various concentrations. Apart from nitrogen, phosphorous, and potassium, cannabis plants can also benefit from nutrients such as:

• Calcium

• Sulphur

• Magnesium

• Manganese

• Boron

• Copper

• Zinc

• Molybdenum

• Iron

GROW LIGHT BASICS

If you've decided to grow indoors, your grow light will serve as the heart of your operation. There are a variety of different grow lights available to you, and you'll want to know which to choose well before you start your grow.

Here are some of the most popular cannabis grow lights available to you:

Compact fluorescent lights (CFLs): These are inexpensive lights commonly used by first-time growers. CFLs lack the power of professional grow lights and usually produce smaller harvests.

Fluorescent Lighting (T5 / T8): T5 and T8 flourescent lights are more apt for growing cannabis. However, these lights usually give off lower light intensities than needed, meaning you'll have to install them very close to the tops of your plants.

LED grow lights: LED lights are the most expensive option available to you. These lights can produce great results and may also help keep your power costs in check. However, they may not be feasible for smaller grows given their price.

Metal Halide (MH) and High Pressure Sodium (HPS): MH and HPS lights are relatively cheap and produce great results, making them one of the most popular options for indoors growers.

PICKING THE RIGHT STRAIN

There are 1000s of cannabis strains out there. Before you start your grow, you'll want to research the different strains out there and choose one that best suits your grow space and skills as a grower.

The difference between strains can be huge, affecting everything from a plant's morphology to the effects of its buds. Make sure you read up on some of the different strains available to you on our strain database and choose something that suits your grow space, skills, and smoking preferences.

KEEP YOUR GROW SECRET

If you're lucky enough to live in an area where cannabis has been legalized, this may not apply to you. If not, mark our words and keep your cannabis grow a secret. Sure, growing your own weed is fun and exciting, and you'll probably want to tell your friends about it. But remember, the repercussions for cultivating cannabis can be huge, so you'll want to keep your grow op on the downlow as much as possible. The last thing you'll want to deal with is an unexpected knock on your door from the police.

MONITOR YOUR PERFORMANCE

When you're new to growing cannabis, it's important you keep tabs on all your hard work. Hence, we always recommend you take the time to document the progress of your grow. How you do so is up to you. A simple option is to take photos of your plants on a weekly basis to document their growth and progress. Alternatively, you may want to keep a grow journal in which you note down specific details about your grow, such as the nutrients you're using, your light schedule, and any events like pest infestations etc.

Documenting the progress of your grow allows you to keep tabs on all the various factors affecting your plants and how you dealt with them. This is especially important for new growers as it allows them to revisit their work and improve their processes. One extra remark on this one: If you grow weed in a place where it is illegal it might be a good idea NOT to monitor your performance. When caught by the police you don't want them to find a notebook with all your grows from the last 5 years including the amounts you harvested in that time. They will use it as proof for sure.

KNOW HOW TO HARVEST

Last but not least, before you start your cannabis grow, you'll want to be sure you know what to do come harvest time.

First of all, you'll want to know the different stages of harvest and how they can affect the potency and effects of your buds. Buds that are harvested earlier, for example, tend to have more uplifting effects, while buds harvested later are said to have more relaxing, sedative-like effects. Plus, you'll also want to know what to do with your buds once it comes time to harvest them. After you've taken your buds from a plant, you'll need to know how to trim, dry, cure, and store them to ensure the best results.

GET GROWING

So, there you have it; a rundown of all you need to know before you start growing your own cannabis. Now that you're up to speed, it's time to order your seeds and get planting!

CANNABIS GROWING METHODS

There are many different ways to grow medical marijuana. Which method is right for you depends upon your circumstances and what you want to invest in time, money and commitment. This guide will give you a good summary of the various methods and a short summary of their advantages and disadvantages.

Any of these methods will yield good results for a dedicated gardener. However, what you get out of it will depend upon what you put into it. A crop is subject to all kinds of threats, ranging from lack of water, to improper fertilizer, to bugs and animals that will eat it. If you really want good, high-grade marijuana you will have to put a little work into it, no matter which method you use.

The first step, of course, is to get some seeds or clones to get you started. Once you obtain these, you have to select a growing method:

Plain Dirt

This is the traditional method of growing anything. Just grow the marijuana as you would any other plant. Use good soil, and make sure that you keep it watered and properly fertilized.

Advantages:

It is usually easier and cheaper than any other method.

You can use standard nursery store fertilizers.

Disadvantages:

Unless you get commercial growing soil, the soil can be of uncertain quality. You could lose a crop or have poor results because the minerals and nutrients in the soil are out of balance.

Yields will probably not be as great as you will get with other methods.

Coco Fiber/Rock Wool

Instead of using soil as a medium to hold the roots, you can use an inert medium — something that does not have the quality problems found with ordinary soil.

Advantages:

Almost as easy as growing marijuana in plain soil.

Better yields than soil.

Almost as cheap and simple as plain soil.

The process is generally cleaner with fewer bugs and mess..

Disadvantages:

Requires special fertilizers which are more expensive.

Requires the purchase of coco fiber. This is not very expensive, but you may have to find a local store that stocks it.

Hydroponics

Hydroponics consists of growing the plants in something such as gravel, with no soil or vegetable matter in the mix. The gravel will be contained in pots or troughs. Water with a light mix of special fertilizers will be either poured through the gravel, or the troughs will be flooded with the fertilizer several times throughout the day.

If you view roots grown in hydroponics versus those grown in plain soil, you will see an immediate difference. While roots grown in soil have a big tap root, the roots grown in hydroponics will have no major tap root, but will consist of a huge bunch of small, clean white hairs.

Advantages:

Much bigger yields than the previous methods.

Cleaner because no soil is used.

Disadvantages:

Costs a lot more because it requires troughs, pumps, and reservoirs to hold the water/fertilizer mixture.

Requires a lot more labor. You will need to monitor pH and nutrient levels to make sure they stay within proper limits.

It takes more equipment. Therefore it may take more room.

Aeroponics

Aeroponics consists of growing roots in plain air. The plants are held in a mesh basket, hanging out in the air, and the water and fertilizer is continuously sprayed over the roots. This method produces roots that are even more amazing than hydroponics.

Advantages:

Fastest growth and biggest yields of all. Results can be spectacular.

Disadvantages:

Costs more than growing in soil because it requires equipment similar to that used in hydroponics.

Requires more labor. In order to get good results, it must be monitored on a daily basis.

Very sensitive to mistakes. You must keep the nutrients and pH in a specific range for optimum results. If the measures of nutrients and pH in your water gets out of limits, you can have really bad results in a big hurry.

Aquaponics

One particular alternative method that has gained popularity goes by the name of Aquaponics. Aquaponics is a combination of two traditional food production techniques: Hydroponics & Aquaculture. The concept of aquaponics is based around the idea of raising fish and growing plants together in one integrated and soil-less system. The fish and the plants form a symbiotic relationship in which the fish are providing the plants with a food source, and the plants are acting as a natural filter to cleanse the water the fish live in. When operated inside a climate-controlled greenhouse, aquaponics systems are capable of producing premium quality, organic plants and fish anywhere, during any time of the year.

The key component to a thriving aquaponics system is the beneficial bacteria responsible for converting fish waste, decaying plant matter, and uneaten food into ammonia and other compounds that are consumed by the plants. This naturally occurring, nitrifying bacteria, inhabit every and all surfaces of your aquaponics system, especially the grow medium in the hydroponics system.

TYPES OF GROW LIGHTS

Fluorescent

Fluorescent grow lights are popular for propagation, early vegetative growth and over-wintering semi-hardy and tender plants. T5 fluorescents are the most modern type. They are available as single, daisy-chainable strips or in panel arrays. Lamps need to be matched to the fixture (high output "HO" or very high output "VHO"). Different spectral distribution lamps are available-most common are "daylight" and "bloom." Daylight lamps are used for propagation, vegetative growth and over-wintering. Bloom lamps are commonly used as side-lighting for larger plants flowering indoors.

High Intensity Discharge (HID)

High Intensity Discharge (HID) grow lights are the most common type of grow light for general purpose indoor applications because they are extremely efficient and capable of producing intense light indoors. Metal Halide "MH" lamps give off a bluish spectrum, perfect for vegetative growth. They also contain some ultra violet radiation "UV" which is useful for combating pests, molds and promoting the production of essential oils in aromatic crops. High Pressure Sodium "HPS" emit a yellow / orange light that simulates the fall sun-perfect for flowering and fruiting. Many growers combine HPS and MH lamps to provide a better overall light spectrum for their plants.

Plasma

Plasma is a relatively new lighting technology which is still proving to be prohibitively expensive for the vast majority of consumers. Plasma grow lights offer higher efficiency than HID, longer lamp life and less depreciation, and improved output spectrum-especially for vegetative growth.

Light Emitting Diode (LED)

LED technology is perhaps one of the quickest developing areas with significant progress occurring on a regular basis. Some early panel LED fixtures entered the horticultural industry with grand claims that didn't match up to reality. The marketplace has now matured somewhat and LED grow lights are beginning to find their place. Many medical marijuana growers use LED grow lights to supplement the spectrum of their existing grow light setup in order to steer plants into generative development (flowering and fruiting).

THE LIFE-CYCLE OF CANNABIS HORTICULTURE

cannabis horticultureThe key to successfully cannabis horticulture is to understand exactly how marijuana produces food and grows healthy. Whether grown indoors or outdoors, the requirements for cannabis horticulture remain the same.

The basic necessities of cannabis are light, air, water, nutrients, a growing medium and heat to create the necessary energy to grow. Growing indoors, the requirements are the same, though it is necessary to be sure that you have the proper light spectrum, carbon dioxide (CO_2) and air circulation for cannabis to grow and thrive.

When you have proper amounts of everything needed for proper cannabis horticulture the result is consistent and optimum levels of growth. Marijuana is normally grown as an annual plant, completing its life cycle within one year so the seeds are planted in the spring and grown throughout the summer. Growing larger and larger until fall, the plants begin to produce flowers and create seeds to continue the full life-cycle of cannabis. In its natural state cannabis horticulture goes through distinct growth stages throughout its life-cycle.

Marijuana Germination

cannabis horticultureIn the germination stage, after about 3 – 7 days, the seedlings sprout white-colored roots and begin to establish their root system in this stage of cannabis horticulture. Soon thereafter they were to grow stems and develop their first few leaves. Moisture, heat, and air are the activators of the seed hormones (cytokinins, gibberellins, and auxins) during the germination life cycle of marijuana seeds. The hormones of the seed reside within the durable outer coating of the seed and the hormone cytokinin triggers cells to form and tells the gibberellins to grow in size. The embryo of the seed expands in size, utilizing the supply of food stored within the seed for growth.

Cannabis Seedling Growth

SproutA single tap-root is produced from the germination of the seed as it grows down through the soil or growing medium and then the root systems begin to branch out. While the roots grow below the surface, the stem branches upward, above the ground in search of the light for its growth.

Tiny rootlets in the root system draw in water and nutrients as the root system develops in size, helping to anchor the plant and create a foundation for its future growth. Seedlings need to receive about 16-18 hours of light for healthy, vigorous growth in the beginning stages of cannabis horticulture.

Marijuana Vegetative Growth

how to grow cannabisDuring this stage of cannabis horticulture the plants need a minimum of 16 hours of light to stay in the vegetative state; though a maximum lighting time of 24 hours a day, 7 days a week can also be used. In cannabis horticulture, as the plant matures, their root systems take on specialized roles – the center, older and more mature roots contain a water transport system that may also store food for the plant.

The tips of the roots extend and push deeper and farther into the soil in search of nutrients and water to supply its growth. These single-celled root hairs are the essential key for the plants to be able to uptake water and nutrients for growth. The roots are extremely delicate and must be handled as quickly, gently, and carefully as possible if doing any kind of transplanting since they are prone to dry up and die very easily if they lack water. They may also be damaged by open air and sunlight if exposed for too long.

Similar to its root system, the cannabis' stem grows and stretches higher and farther to catch more sunlight. In cannabis horticulture the plants will produce nodes and buds along its stem – depending if it is Sativa- or Indica-dominant strain – the nodes will be at varying distances between each node.

The central stem's primary function is to transfer water and nutrients from its delicate root hairs up and throughout the entire cannabis plant. Lateral and side branches continue to branch out to develop buds and for the leaves to capture light.

CANNABIS PRE-FLOWERING

This begin to show around the fourth week into vegetative growth, depending on the strain in cannabis horticulture. It is around this time that you will usually be able to determine the sex of the plant. Between the fourth and sixth node is where you will usually be able to find the pre-flowers of the cannabis plant. The male cannabis plant will develop tiny, smooth, egg-shaped pollen sacks while the female cannabis plant will develop small V-shaped white or pink hairs called pistils.

Sometimes it may be hard to tell which are male and female. If you are unsure then you can grow them for a longer period of time to ensure you are able to correctly identify the plant's sex (male or female). If you want to ensure a seedless crop (sinsemilla), you will want to be sure to remove all males from your crop.

INDOOR CANNABIS PLANT DURING FLOWERING

Indoor growing has become increasingly common over the past decade because of the increased availability of equipment, seeds and instructions on how to cultivate. So-called grow-ops (growing operations, often located in grow houses) are seen by many marijuana enthusiasts as a much cheaper way to gain a steady, higher-quality supply of cannabis. On a larger scale they have proven a viable commercial venture, with some law enforcement agencies finding grow-ops large enough to yield several kilograms of cannabis. More expansive grow-ops are generally more susceptible to detection than smaller operations.

In the UK, so much cannabis is grown in illegal facilities that the UK is an exporter of cannabis. After cannabis as a drug was rescheduled as a Class B drug in 2008 (see below), more people started reporting on their suspicions of illegal operations and in 2009-2010 almost 7000 illegal facilities were found by police in one year. Vietnamese teenagers are trafficked to the United Kingdom and forced to work in these facilities. When police raid them, trafficked victims are typically sent to prison.

Because individual grow light power generally ranges from 250 watts to 1000 watts or more and because the lights remain lit for a long time each day, differences in utility bill costs are a significant security issue. Power companies inform law enforcement if they see a significant increase in power usage relative to a household's previous electricity costs or if power is being stolen by bypassing the meter. Employing energy saving methods is a common way to alleviate this, for instance; switching off light bulbs when leaving rooms, purchasing energy efficient appliances, using TVs or computers less, buying lower power light bulbs and so forth.

Some plants (e.g. cultivars of C. sativa subsp. indica), can give off strong odors as they grow, resulting in detection of illegal growing operations. Growers frequently use carbon scrubbers and ventilation to control odors. This typically involves forcing air from the grow room through a device containing activated carbon, then venting it outdoors. Others use an ozone generator. Ozone reacts with odor molecules in the air, permanently eliminating them. However, ozone can build up to levels that may be hazardous both for grower and plant. As a last resort, keeping windows firmly shut and using strong air fresheners can control smells. Checking outside to see if any smells are emanating from indoors is often a necessary precaution, as many growers become acclimated to the smell, and fail to realize just how pervasive the odor may be. Many store plants in more isolated areas such as a basement or attic to prevent smell detection. Another less common solution is to simply grow a strain with a weaker odor.

Storing plants and lights away from windows and areas that visitor may see is also common, as is keeping the plants in an attic or basement. Some growers, finding this impractical, may cover windows with light-resistant materials. This can solve the problem of escaping bright light but may arouse suspicion amongst neighbors and local residents.

Many cultivators face the risk of fire. Fires normally originate from faulty electrical equipment or wiring. Shoddy fixtures and sockets, improperly grounded equipment, and overloaded circuit breakers are some of the most prevalent causes. Because of the large amount of electricity needed for large-scale cultivation, old or damaged wiring is prone to melt and short. Some commercial growers steal power to hide electricity use, and many do not ensure that their wiring is safe. Many growers adapt light cycles so that the lights are on when they are home and off when they are away.

Another fire hazard is plants making contact with hot HID bulbs. Growers using fluorescent bulbs with reasonable air circulation do not have this problem. Word of mouth can be as much a threat to growers as any of the above issues. Often, a few sentences of conversation overheard can result in a tip-off and thus speedy detection. It is for this reason that many growers are reluctant to talk about their cultivation.

Housing damage

For houses used as grow-ops, the interiors may have received significant structural, electrical and heating system modifications not in accordance with applicable building, natural gas and electrical codes, such as overloaded existing electrical system or a bypass circuit to avoid paying for the electricity required to power the high intensity light bulbs and fans, disconnected furnace venting, or holes in floors and walls for increased airflow. These changes replicate warm, humid climates where hybrid plants flourish and produce high potency cannabis. Such modifications may result in considerable structural damage. Cultivation over a period of time may lead to moisture and toxic mold.

One of the largest such examples was masterminded by a Markham, Ontario real estate agent, John Trac, who turned 54 rented houses into grow-ops; he was convicted and imprisoned.

Contractor and television presenter Mike Holmes said that while houses formerly used for growing cannabis could be bought very cheaply from banks or other owners, repairs and remediation could cost around $100,000 CAD, which may exceed price savings. Holmes noted that in one of his past jobs on Holmes on Homes, he and his crew gutted the entire house after discovering it was a grow-op.

In some municipalities, after the police raid a grow-op house they are required to contact the municipality to ensure that it is put back in good condition before being offered for sale, while real estate agents and sellers may be required by law to disclose that the home had been a grow-op. Home inspectors routinely fail to detect tell-tale signs that a house had been used as a grow-op.

Harvesting, drying and curing

Close-up of a female cannabis bud in flowering stage. White trichomes can be seen coating the surface, which darken as flowering progresses.

There may be different goals when harvesting a plant:

Seeds are harvested when fully developed and often after the accompanying buds have begun to deteriorate.

Hemp grown for fiber is harvested before flowering,

Cannabis grown for cloning is not allowed to flower at all.

Cannabis grown for smoking

A typical indicator that a plant is ready to be harvested for smoking, is when most trichomes have turned cloudy and 5% to 15% of the trichomes have turned a reddish brown/amber.

In general, harvesting consists of drying and curing. Curing is an oxidization and polymerization process which takes place in sealed containers of cannabis, over time.

Dry: Buds placed in a controlled atmosphere for removing moisture content

Cure: Buds stored in sealed non-plastic container and left in dark place

Ripeness is defined as the point where THC and other cannabinoid production has reached maximum levels, but before cannabinoids have begun to degrade/breakdown. This is seen under a 30–60x microscope by examining the trichomes on the flowers. When trichomes are undeveloped they are completely clear. They turn white/cloudy which is when trichomes have max levels of cannabinoids. Eventually trichomes start turning amber/purple/red, which is when cannabinoid content has started to degrade. Harvesting before most trichomes have turned white may reduce the overall potency and efficacy time. Harvesting too late (past 15% amber) produces more of a sleepiness effect as the THC degrades to CBN.

Some growers use a brix to measure "sugar" content.

Drying cannabis buds

The plants are dried at room temperature in a dark space. It is actually optimal to keep the temperature between 60 and 70 °F (16 and 21 °C) because many terpenoids (molecules that are partially responsible for the psychoactive effects but also largely responsible for the odor of the plant) evaporate at temperatures beyond 70 °F (21 °C). This process can take from a few days to two weeks, depending on the size and density of the buds and the relative humidity of the air. Humidity should be kept between 45% and 55% humidity. Higher humidity will create a mold and mildew risk, while lower humidity will cause the material to dry too quickly. If the plant material dries too quickly, some of the chlorophyll will fail to be converted to a different chemical form which will result in a sub-optimal taste and a harsher smoke when combusted and inhaled. Stable temperature preserves cannabinoids well. Some believe flowers should be hung by their stalks, allowing the internal fluids of the plant to remain in the flowers. Others believe the cut stem is simply a handy non-sticky place from which to hang the plant. Roots are removed, and when the stems in the middle of the largest buds can be snapped easily, the plant is considered dry enough to be cured. Drying is done in a dark place, as THC resins deteriorate if exposed to light and the degradation product CBN forms, significantly altering the cannabinoid profile of the dried flowers.

Drying the harvest is generally not considered risky by novice indoor growers of cannabis who would like to assume that they have gotten safely to the end of their "grow" by the time they are harvesting their plants. However, generally speaking most will underestimate the sheer scale of odor produced during the cropping, moving and hanging plants to dry. Indoor growers in areas where cultivation is illegal may consider this an obstacle in their overall efforts as the first three days of drying produces very large amounts of discernible odor (organic molecules) which the grower themself may be desensitised to. These will be evaporating and likely discernible to others anywhere in the vicinity of the general area. In populated areas consideration of containment & concentration (i.e. filters) of odor molecules may be employed to reduce risk. In less populated areas with good air movement dissolution and dispersal techniques for odor management may be employed i.e. ventilation from high points such as a chimney or roof vents. Whatever method is to be employed, novice growers in illegal areas would do well to not underestimate the sheer volume of organic molecules being dissipated into the air when harvesting.

Cannabis is fully dry for "curing" when the moisture level reaches 55–65% RH. A simple way to check this is by closing the cannabis up in an airtight glass container with a hygrometer. The container is stored for 12 hours at 22 °C (72 °F) and the hygrometer checked. 65% and above readings mean the jar needs to be opened for a few hours and then closed up, to allow more moisture to escape. The jar is again checked after 12 hours and the process repeated until a steady 55% is reached.

Curing

Once cannabis is dried to 62%, it is sealed in airtight jars to 'cure.' The minimum time for a cure is 30 days. Some growers even cure as long as six months, while others do not cure at all. As with tobacco, curing can make the cannabis more pleasant to smoke. For the same reasons as when drying, curing jars are stored in a cool, dark place.

Brick weed

Paraguayan Brick weed known as Piedra.

Brick weed is a curing and packaging method of cannabis cultivation that consists in drying the bud for a short period, if at all, and pressing it with a hydraulic press, compacting the whole plant (bud, stems and seeds) into a brick, hence the name brick weed. This method is mainly used in the top cannabis producing countries like Mexico and Paraguay where it is largely exported. Brick weed has a low THC level and less potent aroma and taste.

MARIJUANA FLOWERING

Growing marijuana indoorsIn natural growing environment outdoors, cannabis begins to flower in the fall when the days become shorter. Flowers begin to form during this last stage of growth, where leafy growth within the plant slows and flowers begin to form. The changing of the seasons signal hormone changes within the plant so they go from being in a vegetative state into a flowering or blooming stage of their life-cycle. Seasonal changes and the flowering cycle of cannabis horticulture are in direct correlation to the light spectrum of the sun and the amount of time (or hours) the sun is out each day.

The flowering of cannabis is triggered by 12-hours of darkness and 12-hours of light every 24 hours. When left un-pollinated female flowers to develop without seeds, called 'sinsemilla'. Otherwise, when a female plant is fertilized with male pollen, the female flower buds will begin to develop seeds.

GUIDE ON HOW TO GROW MARIJUANA

First Step in How to Grow Weed: Where to Plant

The absolute first thing to decide is whether you are growing pot indoors or outdoors. Whatever you choose, remember that the smaller the project, the lower the risk. If you're just trying your hand at growing marijuana, start small. Not only are the costs for one plant lower, but it's also easier to take care of one plant instead of ten.

That being said, leave some extra room. When it comes to how to grow pot, you can never tell. If you're lucky, your plant might triple in size, or you might be a super successful grower and move on to cultivating more plants in no time.

Indoor vs. Outdoor Cannabis Cultivation

In general, plants grown outdoors are bigger and, as a result, produce bigger yields. Furthermore, you get to utilize natural light and other elements (free of charge), which means costs are considerably lower. Growing plants indoors, on the other hand, can be a hefty investment to set up, but you have more control in terms of harvest and pest control. There are also legal issues regarding how to grow marijuana outdoors. For example, if you want to grow pot in some states, you have to keep plants hidden from public view, which is not an issue with indoor growing. The biggest difference, however, is that outdoor plants flower only once a year (you plant them in spring and harvest them in fall), whereas if you grow them inside, you can harvest them whenever you want.

The good news is that there is little to no difference in potency and taste (unless you have an extremely sensitive palate for cannabis), so choosing the environment, where and how to grow your own weed, is entirely up to you and the conditions are at your disposal. If you choose the great outdoors, make sure you find a place that has access to plenty of light and enough room for the plant to grow naturally. Also, buy seeds from an outdoor strain, just to make the process a bit easier. And another thing: Outdoor plants need at least 8 hours of direct sunlight per day. So, make sure you choose a location that provides your precious plants with plenty of sunshine!

How to Grow Weed Indoors: What Will You Need?

If indoors is more your style, then let's look over some of the things you'll need to get started.

DECIDE ON A GROW ROOM

You can grow cannabis almost anywhere you want. It can be in a spare room, a closet, the garage, or even a grow tent.

Grow tents are a good choice because they come with many advantages: you can quickly put them up and take them down, they're a cheap indoor grow setup, and some of them even come with extra features (like hydroponic equipment or separate chambers for cloning).

Your grow room doesn't have to be some kind of hi-tech lab, just make sure it is dry and cool, and that you have enough room.

Lighting

One of the great things about growing marijuana inside is you get to control the light. And, thus, the yield and the harvest.

Of all the investment in indoor growing, lighting will probably set you back the most. However, it is also one of the most important factors in how to grow marijuana indoors and produce a yield rich both in quality and quantity.

What Kind of Lights Can You Use?

HID (High-Intensity Discharge) is most widely used because they are incredibly powerful, but quite cheap and easy to set up. The two main types of HID lights are Metal Halide and High-Pressure Sodium. HID lights produce a lot of heat (note that you will need air-cooled reflector hoods too), which can run up quite an electricity bill.

It is costly, but using HID lamps will make the process of how to grow cannabis easier in the long-run, especially if you use smaller MH/HPS grow lights.

LEC (Light Emitting Ceramic). This type of bulb provides more natural light, it is less conspicuous, and it emits considerable levels of UV light, which is known to up trichome production.

LED lights are among the top choices for growing weed. They are more expensive (good quality LED lights can cost ten times more than an HID setup), but it might be worth paying a few extra bucks as LED lights last longer and are generally more efficient when it comes to how to grow pot indoors.

Fluorescent grow lights. These kinds of lights are perfect for small-time growers because they are cheaper and easier to set up, and they don't need a cooling system due to the small amount of heat they produce.

The biggest downside would be efficiency (they generate almost 30% less light) and space (you would need bigger lights to achieve the same results as HPS bulb).

Extra Tips

The optimal lighting for a cannabis plant would be a 400-watt bulb for the vegetative stage and a 600-watt lamp for the flowering phase. Another tip on how to grow marijuana: invest in a timer to keep the process consistent.

Also, make sure that the light covers all of your plants as light exposure is crucial to the size and potency of your buds.

Modern Times

There are now modern systems that incorporate lights, hydration systems, and fans, as well as some that come equipped with smartphone technology and a camera so you can keep an eye on your precious plants wherever you are. Indoor growing systems and tech sure have come a long way from a bulb and a container in the corner of your spare room.

Air, Temperature, and Humidity

Cannabis may have some magical effects on your brain and body, but it is a plant, like all others, and it needs a steady flow of air to grow.

This means that you need an intake for fresh air and an exhaust for stale air, as well as a fan to keep the air moving. If you're worried about how to grow weed at home because of the smell, maybe add a carbon filter to the fan. Filters will also help you regulate the temperature in the grow room, which should be between 70–85°F.

Humidity is another critical factor to consider. Leaves aspirate and release moisture (as leaves are known to do), which can create a problem as too much moisture in the air is the perfect breeding ground for pests and mold. On top of that, drier environments result in more resin, and who doesn't want that?

Now that you're all set up, let's start growing weed.

CHOOSE A GROW MEDIUM

Soil

Apart from being the most traditional choice, it is also the easiest, making it ideal for beginners. You can use any potting soil provided it doesn't contain artificial extended-release fertilizer, which is not good for cannabis cultivation.

Super-soil is possibly the best soil for weed because, in this case, you won't need any extra nutrients. Or you can just go for an organic potting mix, which is available in most stores. Combine this with the right nutrients, and you're all set.

How to grow a weed plant and choose the best soil for cannabis?

The right soil should be airy enough for the oxygen to reach the plant's roots and have a balanced pH level (between 6.5 and 7.5). Soil with high acidity levels increases the chances of growing a male cannabis plant. An outcome no one is really thrilled about.

Soilless

Another popular grow medium is the soilless, hydroponic medium, i.e., a process in which the roots absorb nutrients through osmosis. This is useful as it allows for faster growth and bigger buds. Still, it requires more precision.

How to grow hydroponic weed?

Some of the materials you can use include mineral wool, coco coir, perlite, and pebbles, although there is a lot more to choose from. These materials can be used both in hydroponic setups or individual containers, and they can also be mixed and matched to get the best possible results. Some people choose to grow cannabis with roots suspended in the air or in a tank with water, but as you may suppose, these are not the most common of growing mediums.

A highly recommended way to grow pot for beginners is coco coir.

Why and how to grow marijuana with coco coir?

It is not expensive and it fits both indoor and outdoor growing methods. It also holds water well and allows the cannabis plant to take in more nutrients and oxygen as it uses fibrous coconut husks instead of potting soil. In addition, throwing in too many nutrients will not have as devastating an impact as with other growing methods.

A word on containers

You can use "smart pots" or plain old gallon buckets, just make sure that there are holes at the bottom to help boost airflow and provide proper drainage.

ADD NUTRIENTS AND WATER

Unless you opt for super soil, you'll need nutrients to ensure that your cannabis plant grows up to be strong and healthy. The same goes for hydroponic mediums, although if you are planning on using any of these, you will need special kinds of nutrients.

Most nutrients are available in a two-part liquid: one for the vegetative state and another for the flowering state. So, just follow the instructions on the label telling you how to grow weed outside, as well as indoors, and everything will go smoothly. The most important thing to remember about feeding your pot plant is not to use too many nutrients in the beginning, or you'll burn your plant. This is actually a fairly common mistake, especially among novice growers. Raise the dosage of nutrients only if you see that your plant really needs it, for instance, if the lower leaves are turning yellow (unless it's 2 or 4 weeks before harvest time when this is normal).

Another thing to be cautious about in terms of how to grow marijuana outside is the quality of water you use on your pot plant. Water in certain parts of the world can have high amounts of minerals impacting the intake of nutrients. Next, there is the hardness of the water or its pH value. 6.0–7.0 pH for soil and 5.5–6.5 pH for hydroponics should be good enough for growing marijuana. If you don't have that kind of pH value where you live, you can use purified or RO water, or add some Cal/Mag supplements.

CHOOSE THE RIGHT STRAIN

Picking the right strain can be a challenge since there are so many to choose from, but it is also one of the more exciting parts of growing your own weed.

Male and Female Marijuana Plants

In the world of cannabis, it is the female weed plant that grows big, seedless buds full of THC. Male plants, on the other hand, pollinate the female ones, filling their flowers with seeds. A small tip on how to grow good weed: seeded flowers don't qualify as high-grade cannabis, so it's best to keep the male plants away from the females. Growers usually have a male marijuana plant if they are trying to breed a new pot strain or if they need the seeds for another crop.

How to tell if your plant is male or female before flowering?

This can be a bit tricky, so you should look at the guide and photos of male/female plants.

The safest choice would be to buy feminized cannabis seeds. Or use clones as with cuttings you'll definitely get a female plant.

How Many Seeds Do You Need to Grow a Plant?

Depending on the germination rate and the number of plants you want to grow, you'll need about three regular or two feminized seeds for one pot plant.

Choose a Strain

When growing weed, you can go for Indica, Sativa, or auto-flowering strains.

Sativa strains are known to grow tall and develop long buds, whereas Indicas are shorter, do better in the cold, and produce dense buds. Sativas and Indicas also have different effects, so base your decision on what you'll use the weed for. Or just use a hybrid — there are plenty nowadays. Speaking of which…

How to Grow Marijuana Inside and Outside with Auto-Flowering Strains

These strains start flowering automatically, i.e., they don't need light schedules to move from the vegetative to the flowering stage!

Auto-flowering strains are usually a mix of Indica and Sativa, they are small and compact, and they provide fast and rapid results. Some of the downsides of auto-flowering plants are that you can't clone them, and they sometimes produce lower yields with less THC. Still, auto-flowering strains are highly recommended among growers, especially newbies who find it challenging to manage the light cycle during the flowering phase. How long does it take to grow weed with auto-flowering strains? Typically, these strains flower in 3 weeks to a month after the seed is planted, unlike other strains that can take months to bloom.

GERMINATING SEEDS

Following this step, you will need to make a decision. To use or not to use seeds and clones? And what's the main difference between the two?

Clones

Clones are basically cuttings from a mature marijuana plant that can be replanted and grown. Sounds simple enough, right? Actually, the process of how to grow marijuana from clones can be more complicated, especially for first-timers. Clones can come with genetic issues, and they are very sensitive when replanted, so they need a lot of care and attention. Possibly the biggest benefit of using clones is the certainty of getting a female weed plant. On top of that, the flowering process is faster, especially when growing marijuana outdoors. Nevertheless, many growers say that they take pride and joy in growing a marijuana plant from the earliest stages.

How to Grow Weeds From Seeds?

One way to germinate your seeds is to put them directly in the soil, or whatever grow medium you are using. Not only is this the easiest and least stressful method for both the seeds and the growers but it is also the most natural, and we all know that "natural" is synonymous with "top-quality."

How to plant seeds?

The seeds should be planted knuckle-deep, the soil should be moist, but not too wet, and the temperature should be around 75°F (23°C).

How to grow marijuana from seed? Wait for 3 to 7 days for tiny sprouts to appear, and that's it! You're on your way to getting a full-grown cannabis plant.

Another way to germinate seeds is to use the paper towel method.

What you need to do is put the seeds between two moist paper towels until the seeds begin to sprout (this could take anywhere between a day and a week). As soon as the small sprouts emerge, put the seeds in the soil, cover the top and make sure your plants get plenty of light, water, and heat.

VEGETATIVE STAGE

During the vegetative phase, which begins once your cannabis plant starts growing new leaves and stems, your plant will focus solely on growing big, but not on growing buds. To help it along the way you need to provide proper care and nourishment. If you are growing marijuana outdoors, make sure the plant gets direct sunlight for the better part of the day, ideally between 10 AM and 4 PM. Growing plants indoors is a different story. One of the biggest benefits when it comes to how to grow marijuana at home is that growers can keep the plant in the vegetative stage for as long they want. Putting lights on a timer and exposing the plant to a minimum of 18 hours of light every day will trick your cannabis plant into thinking it's growing time and stay in the vegetative stage for longer.

The longer the plant stays in the vegetative stage, the taller it gets, and of course, this means a bigger yield as well. Smaller plants may start to flower after less than a month. However, the typical length of this phase is 3 to 5 weeks.

How to Grow Bigger Buds Outdoors and Indoors

It goes without saying that you can let nature take its course, but there are some things during the vegetative stage you can do to make sure that your plants produce bigger and more potent buds.

Stress Training

Both low-stress training and Super Cropping involve bending down the branches, so the plant grows wider, instead of growing upwards. Be careful not to snap off the branches as you tie them down, especially with outdoor plants, to get bigger buds in the flowering stage.

Pruning

Not everyone feels the same way about more advanced outdoor growing techniques, such as pruning. However, there are many growers out there who believe that this technique is one of the best ways to achieve an optimal yield. There are three pruning methods you can try:

Topping — cutting off the top of the plant makes it grow bushier and wider.

Fimming — This is similar to topping, however, here you just cut off a little bit of the top. It's less traumatic than topping, and it increases cola yields.

Lollipopping — This technique removes the side, low branches of the cannabis plant allowing all the nutrients to get to the top.

FLOWERING STAGE

Once your pot plant receives 12 hours of darkness every day, it will start producing buds. You must provide 12 hours of complete, uninterrupted darkness. Light leaks will stress and confuse your plant, making it revert to the vegetative stage or turn it into a hermaphrodite, which results in pollination and seedy buds. If you're growing marijuana outdoors, your plant should start flowering naturally as the days get shorter.

How long does it take to grow marijuana in this phase? The blooming stage typically lasts for 8 to 10 weeks and goes on until it's time for harvest. This phase is when you can definitely tell if you have a male marijuana plant or a female, not to mention it is the stage when the plant is most vulnerable, so keeping a close eye on its growth is crucial.

Exposing your plants to enough light and air during this phase can also boost your buds, the indoor and outdoor grow guide to a bigger yield says. A lot of growers "flush" their cannabis plant by giving it plain water the last two weeks before harvest to prevent a nutrient build-up. But the most important thing is not to harvest too soon! Yes, we know you're eager to sample what you've grown, but harvesting your plant too early is a sure way to get lower yields.

HARVESTING

The best (and right) time to harvest is when the trichomes on your pot plant start to turn white, but before they become entirely amber. According to one of the many High Times growing tips, if you want a more lethargic stone, harvest when trichomes are mostly amber (80–90%).

If you want a broader cannabinoid profile, then begin harvest when the trichomes are 60–80% brown, but If you are looking for more THC, cut the buds when 70% of them grow darker.

DRYING AND CURING

After the harvest comes trimming, drying, and curing. It takes about a week for the buds to dry, depending on how humid the area is. Once they dry, place the buds in jars to cure them so that the extra liquid is completely removed. A small tip on how to grow and cure weed buds: use opaque jars and open them once or twice a day to prevent mold from forming. The curing process should take about four weeks, after which you will have some nice, high-quality buds to give you that perfect hit!

PEST MANAGEMENT

Both indoor and outdoor growers are likely to confront issues regarding pests. Indoor growers have problems with pests, they can be brought in by hitchhiking on humans or through open exposure to the outdoors. The most common insect pest found on above ground plant parts, leaves, flowers and stems, include aphids, thrips, mites and loopers. Below ground pests that feed on the roots can also be present and include fungus gnats and root aphids. Root aphids, namely the rice root aphid can be particularly problematic due to its high reproductive rate and discrete habitat. Several plant diseases may also be prevalent and including bud rot, powdery mildew and root rot. If any of these pests are caught too late, eradication of many destructive species may prove futile unless all infected plants are removed from the space and sterilization methods employed.

Organic and inorganic pest controls

In any case (indoor or outdoor), experienced growers recommend caution when using chemical pesticides, for they may have toxic effects on the environment, the plants themselves and in turn cannabis consumers. As a general rule, experts mandate the deployment of pesticides clearly marked as "safe to use on food crops." However, the EPA has not registered any pesticides for use on cannabis, making the use of any pesticide on cannabis federally illegal.

Substances that have been used and considered to induce little or no harm include:

Pyrethrins: Organic and very effective, although sometimes hard to find. Often expensive because of high production cost.

Azadirachtin: Meets most criteria to be classified as natural insecticide. Biodegradable, non-toxic to mammals. Usually cheaper and easier to find than pyrethrins.

Substances used on cannabis but unknown if harm could occur:

• Avermectins such as Abamectin

• Atrazine

• Bifenthrin

• Copper sulfate

• Diazinon

• Etoxazole

• Imidacloprid

• Myclobutanil

• Permethrin

• Spinosad

• Spiromesifen

• Plant training

This indoor cannabis plant has not been trained and is growing in the natural Christmas tree shape that is common for untrained cannabis indica.

The modification of a plant's growth habit is called training. Indoor cultivators employ many training techniques to encourage shorter plants and denser canopy growth. For example, unless the crop is too large to be extensively pruned, cultivators remove adventitious growth shoots, often called suckers, that are near the bottom of the plant and/or receive little light and will produce poor quality buds. Some cultivators employ plant training techniques to increase yields indoors:

Topping

Topping is the removal of the top of the apical meristem (dominant central stem), called the apex or terminal bud, to transfer apical dominance (the tendency for the apex to grow more rapidly than the rest of the plant) to the shoots emanating from the two nodes immediately beneath the pruning cut. This process can be repeated on one or both of the two new meristems, when they become apically dominant, with the same results. This process can actually be repeated nigh infinitely, but over-diffusion of apical dominance produces smaller, lower quality buds, so it is usually done no more than a few times. Topping also causes more rapid growth of all of the branches below the cut while the plant heals.

Pinching

These indoor cannabis plants were trained to grow flat in order to take better advantage of the grow lights and increase yields.

Pinching (also called "FIMing") is similar to topping in that it causes lower branches to grow more rapidly, but the apical meristem maintain apical dominance, which is especially useful if the plant has already been topped. Pinching is performed by firmly pinching the apical meristem(s) so as to substantially damage vascular and structural cells but without totally breaking the stem. This causes lower limbs to grow more rapidly while the pinched tissue heals, after which time the stem resumes apical dominance.

LST'ing

LST stands for Low Stress Training and is another form of supercropping, many times referred to as LST super-cropping. This technique involves bending and tying the plants branches to manipulate the plant into a more preferred growth shape. This method of training works very well for indoor growers who need to illuminate their plants using overhead lights. Since light intensity greatly diminishes with increased distance (Inverse-square law), LST'ing can be used to keep all growth tips (meristems) at the same distance from the light and can achieve optimal light exposure. LST can be used in conjunction with topping, since topping increases axial growth (side shoots). Topping is often done a few weeks before beginning LST'ing. The training works by changing the distribution of hormones—more specifically auxins—in the plant. LST'ing resembles the training of grape vines into their support lattices. Outdoor gardeners also employ training techniques to keep their plants from becoming too vertical.

SOG

In contrast to the "Screen of Green" method, Sea of Green (or SOG) growing depends on the high density of plants (as high as 60 per square metre or 6 per square foot) to create uniformity in the crop. In this technique, which is often grown in hydroponic media, only the colas of the plants are harvested. Containers are used to enforce the geometric distribution of flowers and plant material, as well as their exposure to lighting and atmosphere. Sea of green is popular with commercial cultivators, as it minimizes the amount of time a plant spends in vegetative stage, and allows very efficient light distribution, keeping the plants much closer to the lights than when grown to full size.

SCROG

SCROG, short for SCReen Of Green, is an advanced training technique for cultivating cannabis, mainly indoors. Closely resembles SOG (or Sea Of Green) with the difference being that SCROG uses extensive training to produce the same field of bud effect with only one plant. Medical growers may find this a helpful technique to maximize harvest if they are only allowed a certain number of plants. A screen such as chicken wire is hung over plants so that the tips of branches are kept at the same level. This allows even light distribution to all of the nodes/bud sites. Once the flowering stage begins, the flower tips reach through the wire and are at relatively equal distances from the light source.

Vegetative state: The plant should remain in the vegetative state until 70 to 80 percent of the net is full. As a branch reaches 7.5 to 10 centimetres (3–4 in) above the wire it is pulled back under the wire and so trained to grow horizontally until flowering. Because of the amount of plant required to fill the net, the vegetative period may require longer than normal to be ready for flowering.

Timing: Timing is vital to the success of a SCROG grow. If the net is not full at harvest, valuable space has been wasted. If the net is too full then the buds will be too crowded to develop properly. Knowing how a plant grows can help to visualize when to flower for maximum effect.

www.ingramcontent.com/pod-product-compliance
Lightning Source LLC
Chambersburg PA
CBHW020512160726
47991CB00007B/2911